Everything is Ice Cream

A Tale of an Old Man and His Tongue

CHET FESTIVE

Published by Bombardier Books
An Imprint of Post Hill Press
ISBN: 979-8-88845-465-7

Post Hill Press
New York • Nashville
posthillpress.com

Printed in Canada
1 2 3 4 5 6 7 8 9 10

In a land very near here,
a short time ago,

There resided a ruler
named President Joe.

He was old, nearly ancient,
with thin, wrinkly skin

And his memory wasn't
what once it had been.

He was very forgetful,
of who people were
Or of what he was doing—
he just wasn't sure!

But the one thing he
practically never forgot
Was he really liked ice
cream! He liked it a lot!

He had liked it for years,
since the time he was young—
How it tasted so sweet,
how it felt on his tongue.

He loved strawberry,
cookie dough, mint
chocolate chip,
Even uncommon flavors,
like licorice whip.

On a typical day, between
meetings and calls
He'd escape from his office
and wander the halls,

Asking people he saw but
whose names he'd misplaced
If they knew of some ice
cream he might like to taste.

They would point, very
helpfully, in the direction
Where Joe might acquire
his favorite confection.

So that's where he shuffled,
this chief of the nation,
And saw there a lady
with brown coloration.

He knew that he knew her!
He snuck up behind.
She was holding and eating
a treat of some kind.

Could that something be ice
cream? He needed to know.
She would surely be willing
to share with old Joe.

After all, they were close!
They'd been on the same ticket!
He needed to try it!
He just had to lick it!

"Excuse me," she said,
"but it's terribly rude
When you sneak up behind
me and slurp at my food."

"...which is awful!" said Joe.
"It's incredibly bad!
Why, that ice cream's the worst
that I ever have had!"

"This is called a kebab, Joe!
It's meat on a stick!
It's not ice cream at all, and
it's not meant to lick!"

So she cut off the part that
he'd licked with a knife,

Then Joe spotted a woman
he saw was his wife.

She was less old than Joe
was, and not very brown,
And she dressed in the style
of a much younger clown.

On her plate was a dish of
a green sort of mound...
...like pistachio ice cream, in
scoops that were round!

With a speed that belied his
advancement in years
Joe took quite a large lick...
then his eyes filled with tears!

"This is mushy and spicy!
It's not even cold!
I'm deporting wherever this
ice cream was sold!"

"Your obsession with ice
cream is out of control!
And I'm not eating ice cream!
It's called gwack-a-mole!"

"Do you mean guacamole?"
Old Joe was confused
At this odd appellation
his wife had just used.

"Well, however you say
it, I want you to know
That I bought it made fresh
from a small body glow!

"What I mean is dog
bangles! I'm trying to say
It's a bagel dough...Gouda-
boy...dad-bod-g'day!"

"It's pagoda," said Joe, with a shake of his head,

"And I don't want Chinese food, but ice cream instead!"

So old Joe left his wife, whose
Chinese was so poor,
Then he went to his son's room
and knocked on his door.

There was nobody in there,
which wasn't abnormal.
These living arrangements
were rather informal.

His globetrotting son would
for weeks disappear
Then, when journalists called,
he would hide away here!

And he often would bring
back a suitcase of cash,
Thus could easily purchase
his own ice cream stash.

So with that thought in mind,
this decrepit old geezer
Began searching 'round for
his son's secret freezer.

He didn't find ice cream,
but saw, with a smile,
A mountain of sugar,
in one giant pile!

Old Joe couldn't help it! His
sweet tooth was aching!
And here was an answer,
right there for the taking!

It wasn't quite ice cream,
but that was alright.
So he buried his face and
he took a big bite!

No, not ice cream, nor sugar,
but to Joe's surprise

Something magical changed
right before his old eyes!

The whole world turned to ice cream! The windows, the doors,

All the furniture, too, and the carpet and floors.

There was softserve and
sundaes, sorbet and gelato.
He'd just hit the jackpot!
He'd just won the lotto!

He licked every surface!
It tasted exquisite!
His son would be thrilled that
he'd stopped for a visit!

The ice cream was everywhere,
scoops upon scoops!
There were singles and doubles
and infinite groups!

All the staff he employed,
once in suits or in skirts,
Were performing their duties
as frozen desserts.

Then a large ice cream sandwich,
in white and in black
(Joe would save him for later,
an afternoon snack)

Said, "A shrill, angry girl has
sailed in on her yacht
And insists that she tell you
the earth is too hot."

"We shall see her this moment!"
Joe giggled with glee.

"Oh, I wonder what flavor
of ice cream she'll be!"

He was taken to meet his
delicious young guest
Who exclaimed in an accent,
"I'm here to protest!"

"You are killing our planet!
You use too much power!
You must stop your engines!
You must stop this hour!"

Poor Joe wasn't certain to
what she referred
But she looked like she tasted
of sweet lemon curd.

"Should we talk about ice cream?
Is that why you're here?"
"What's to say about ice cream?"
she growled with a sneer

"There won't be any ice cream!
The ice cream will boil!
We'll burn to a crisp
if we keep using oil!"

"Oh, don't be so silly,"
said Joe with a wink,
"For the earth is much colder
than you seem to think!"

"The whole world's made of
ice cream, you have to admit,
And you're standing right there
and not melting one bit!"

Then, before she could finish
her cry of "HOW DARE-"

He had licked her whole face
from her chin to her hair!

With a smile of delight, he
skipped down to the pool
Where the ice cream reporters
were, tasty and cool.

They were writing in notebooks
and talking in phones
And their heads were all ice
cream! Their bodies were cones!

He had too much to sample
and no time to chat,

So he licked every face
while they awkwardly sat.

Then he scampered away
to a VIP meeting,

Excited to find out what
next he'd be eating!

There were royals from England,
a prince and his bride,
And the little French
president standing beside,

And a large Georgian lady
who'd lost all her races.
They all looked so yummy
with ice cream for faces!

And last was a monk with
a shiny bald head
Like a human-sized popsicle,
yellow and red.

No time for "How are you?"
No time for "What's kicking?"
Old Joe couldn't help it!
He just started licking!

He started by tasting the
British confections
Whose famous good manners
would give no objections.

He tasted the ginger
in every last curl,
And the wife was vanilla
and chocolate swirl!

And the leader of France
was a chilled macaron!
And the lady from Georgia
was butter pecan!

And the last was the monk,
who stood patiently waiting.
Joe stared at him hungrily,
mouth salivating.

Joe thought that his colors
looked cherry or peachy,
Or something exotic, like
mango and lychee.

He tasted delicious!
Joe's lips gave a smack.
Then the monk, unexpectedly,
licked him right back!

Joe was stunned by that tongue
that came out of the blue,
Then he asked, in amazement...
"Am I ice cream, too?"

"We are all of us ice cream,"
the monk calmly said,
"From the tips of your toes to
the top of your head!"

"You've discovered a secret,
found out on your own,
That the world's rich and
powerful always have known:

"That the world's population
is here to be tasted!

With more than eight billion,
no time must be wasted!"

Now Joe, with the monk and
a few wealthy friends,

Have a wonderful world
where dessert never ends!

Every person they meet,
every girl, every guy,

Every baby and child
is ice cream to try!

If you've wondered at times, if
you've ever had doubt,

Why they're sniffing, they're licking,
their tongue's hanging out,

They're just sampling flavors—
perhaps something new!

On that subject...
...excuse me...